School Jokes

Joe King

Abdo Kids Junior
is an Imprint of Abdo Kids
abdobooks.com

abdobooks.com

Published by Abdo Kids, a division of ABDO, P.O. Box 398166, Minneapolis, Minnesota 55439.
Copyright © 2022 by Abdo Consulting Group, Inc. International copyrights reserved in all countries.
No part of this book may be reproduced in any form without written permission from the publisher.
Abdo Kids Junior™ is a trademark and logo of Abdo Kids.

Printed in China

102021

012022

THIS BOOK CONTAINS
RECYCLED MATERIALS

Photo Credits: Getty Images, iStock, Shutterstock

Production Contributors: Teddy Borth, Jennie Forsberg, Grace Hansen

Design Contributors: Candice Keimig, Pakou Moua

Library of Congress Control Number: 2021940307
Publisher's Cataloging-in-Publication Data

Names: King, Joe, author.

Title: School jokes / by Joe King

Description: Minneapolis, Minnesota : Abdo Kids, 2022 | Series: Abdo kids jokes | Includes online resource.

Identifiers: ISBN 9781098209209 (lib. bdg.) | ISBN 9781644946343 (pbk.) | ISBN 9781098209902 (ebook)
    | ISBN 9781098260262 (Read-to-Me ebook)

Subjects: LCSH: Jokes--Juvenile literature. | Wit and humor--Juvenile literature. | Schools--Juvenile
    literature.

Classification: DDC 818.602--dc23

Table of Contents

School Jokes

How do bees get to school?

On a school buzz!

Why did they stop giving tests at the zoo?

Because it was full of cheetahs!

4

HA! HA!
Why are fish so smart?
Because they live in schools!
WHEN'S LUNCH?
5

What is a snake's favorite subject in school?

Hissssssstory.

What is a witch's favorite subject in school?

Spelling!

6

What do planets like to listen to?
Nep-tunes!
AAH!
ROCK-et & roll!
7

Why did the math book
look sad?

Because it has a lot of problems.

What do you need to get
into high school?

A ladder.

What did the calculator say to the math students?
You can count on me!
HA + HA
9

What's the difference between
a teacher and a train?

The teacher says, "Throw out that gum!"
The train says, "Chew, chew!"

Why did the square and
triangle go to **PE** class?

To stay in shape!

Why did the teacher put on sunglasses?
Because her students were so bright!
THAT'S A SMART JOKE!

Why did the nose want to
stay home from school?

He was tired of getting picked on!

Why is 2+2=5 like your
left foot?

It's not right.

Why did the new student steal a chair from the classroom?
Because the teacher told her to take a seat.
LOL!
LOL!
LOL!
13

Which bet can't be won?

An Alphabet.

How many letters are in
the alphabet?

11! T-H-E A-L-P-H-A-B-E-T.

14

What do Santa's helpers learn in school?

The elfabet!

15

What object is king of the classroom?

The ruler!

Where did the pencil go on vacation?

Pennsylvania!

What did the sharpener say to the pencil when it talked for too long?

Get to the point!

17

Where do people learn to
make ice cream?

In sundae school.

Why was the broom late
for school?

He over swept.

18

How did Benjamin Franklin feel when he discovered electricity?

Shocked!

OH!
OUCH

Watt did I expect?

19

What advice did the

librarian give to the student?

Believe in yourshelf!

What do librarians take with

them when they go fishing?

Bookworms.

What happens when a lot of books jump into the ocean at once?

A title wave!

HAH!
HAH!
HAH!

Joke-Telling Tips!

• Know your audience

• Timing is everything

• Confidence is key

• Go out on a high note!

22

Glossary

pun

a joke using a word that sounds like a different word or has another meaning. Examples from this book are "cheetah" (cheater) and "sundae" (Sunday).

PE

short for Physical Education. A course teaching sports, exercise, and the care of the human body.

school

a large group of the same kind of fish or sea animals.

Index

Visit **abdokids.com** to access crafts, games, videos, and more!